Simple Food Recipe For Cats

Firat .C Peel

Introduction

This is an indispensable guide for cat owners who want to provide their feline friends with nutritious and delicious homemade meals. It delves into the essential aspects of preparing cat food at home, emphasizing the importance of providing balanced and safe nutrition for your beloved pets.

One of the key strengths of this cookbook is its thorough exploration of the fundamentals of homemade cat food. It begins by explaining the basics, laying the foundation for cat owners to understand the rationale behind homemade meals. By doing so, it empowers pet owners to make informed choices about their cats' diets, taking their health and well-being into consideration.

The cookbook doesn't shy away from discussing the potential risks associated with homemade cat food, which is a crucial aspect of responsible pet ownership. It highlights the importance of understanding these risks and provides valuable insights on how to mitigate them. This focus on safety and well-being ensures that cat owners can confidently provide homemade meals without compromising their pets' health.

The practical aspect of preparing homemade cat food is also addressed comprehensively. It provides a list of essential tools and equipment, ensuring that cat owners are well-prepared to embark on their culinary journey for their feline companions. This attention to detail, from knife sharpeners to label makers, demonstrates a commitment to making the cooking process as seamless as possible.

Furthermore, the cookbook offers a thorough nutrient breakdown, emphasizing the importance of providing cats with a well-balanced diet. It goes beyond simple recipes and encourages cat owners to understand the nutritional content of their homemade cat food, ensuring that their pets receive the essential nutrients they need for a healthy life.

Transitioning from commercial cat food to homemade meals can be challenging, and the cookbook recognizes this. It provides practical tips for a smooth transition, allowing cat owners to make the change gradually and with minimal disruption to their cats' routines.

The heart of the cookbook lies in its collection of recipes, categorized by meat type. Whether you're preparing chicken, beef, turkey, rabbit, or fish-based meals for your cat, you'll find a variety of recipes that cater to different tastes and preferences. These recipes are designed to be both nutritious and appealing to your feline friends, ensuring they look forward to mealtime.

Additionally, the cookbook delves into the realm of cat treats, providing an overview of homemade treats and even discussing dehydrated meat treats. This section adds an extra layer of delight for cat owners who want to pamper their pets with tasty and healthy snacks.

In conclusion, this book is an invaluable resource for cat owners who want to take their pets' nutrition into their own hands. With its emphasis on safety, nutrition, and practicality, it guides cat owners through the process of preparing homemade meals with confidence. Whether you're a novice or an experienced cook, this cookbook ensures that your feline companions enjoy delicious and healthy homemade food.

Contents

THE BASICS OF HOMEMADE CAT FOOD

Maybe you have made homemade cat food before, and you're just looking for new recipes or support. Maybe you just adopted a cat, and you realize the questionable ingredients in that bag of food they came with and how you don't want to feed your new friend that.

Perhaps you are just like I was, dealing with a cat that is going through health issues and desperately looking for a way to ease its pain and discomfort. Even if your cat is healthy now, feeding them a healthy, balanced diet of fresh foods and vegetables can help keep them that way for longer.

Whatever your reasons, I'm glad you are here. These are the basics of homemade food for your cats.

Misconceptions About Homemade Pet Food

There are so many misconceptions about homemade cat food and a lot of misconceptions floating around online and on discussion boards. Before this book dives deep into the finer points of creating meals for your cats, it will touch on the many misconceptions you may find in your food journey and the actual truth behind it all.

"Isn't making my own pet food way more expensive?"

This is probably the most common question I get from pet owners learning more about creating their own pet meals. "Isn't it crazy expensive?"

The honest answer is no, but it's also about value. If I were to feed my cats generic, off-brand food, the bottom of the barrel stuff, then sure. I could spend less on their daily meals. A lot less, maybe. But if you consider the comparable products on the market, the higher-end foods with real food and real ingredients (no byproducts or 'meal'), then it's really not all that much more expensive.

I also buy my pet's food ingredients in bulk and freeze what we're not using at the moment. Getting things on sale and stocking up brings the price way down. I'm not feeding DD or Babs the $25/lb. salmon from Whole Foods, after all! I love them, of course, but there are limits.

In short: yes, it's far more expensive than paying for the cheapest food on the market. The price won't compare. However, it's not nearly as expensive as the raw or 'real' foods on the market and often comes in cheaper than the 'nice' dry kibble you can buy at your local pet store.

"Is making my cat's food something only crazy cat people do?"

No! So many people give me a questionable look when I tell them that I make my own cat's food. "Oh, you're one of those owners."

That is completely unfair and, honestly, kind of a hurtful stereotype.

My life does not revolve around my cats, although I understand the fact that I wrote a book about them undercuts that statement. The truth is, though, it doesn't take all that much in the week to prep my cat's food. I don't spend nights and weekends cuddled up on the couch with them, and yes, I have friends and a life outside of them.

No, people who choose to make their cat's food are not just crazy cat ladies or lads. I promise that if you go down this path with your cat, you will not be forced to join the Crazy Cat Society.

"Can I just toss chicken and rice in a bowl and call it a day?"

Oh my goodness, no! Please don't do this!

Many people seem to think that making cat food is easy because their cats will eat almost anything, so as long as they toss some food in a bowl each day, they are covered. This is actually very dangerous.

Just like with any animal, cats have specific dietary needs. If you are going to feed your cat homemade food, you need to ensure that it is properly balanced with nutrients and meat, so they have all of their needs met. If you neglect to provide your cat with the full spectrum of nutrients in their meals, you can end up making them sick in the long run, which is obviously not the goal.

"Is it hard to hit my cat's nutrient needs?"

It can be if you don't know what you are doing!

That is where this book can help. There is a whole section doing a deep dive into the nutrients that every cat needs to live their best life and how to best give it to them. Each recipe later in the book also details exactly what to put into the meals to give your pets what they need.

As long as you understand what your cat's nutrient needs are, it isn't hard to hit them.

Why Homemade?

Great question!

The biggest reason is that we love our pets. More than ever, people treat their pets not as an accessory or something to keep around but as family. And as your family, you want the best for them. What you feed them matters.

Some studies have suggested that dry food isn't great for a cat's digestive system. It doesn't have nearly the moisture that a cat should be consuming with its meals, and it's full of carbs, additives, and questionable preservatives.

When you make the food, you know exactly what is in it. You don't have to worry about recalls (does anyone else remember in the late 2000s when a ton of pet food was recalled?!), about spoilage, about the quality of their meals… you're making it yourself.

If you have a picky eater, you know how hard it can be to get them to eat the same thing again and again. For many cats, they get bored. Think about how small their life is, honestly. Add in eating the same dry, bland food day in and out? That isn't a good way to live.

By creating their meals, you can change what they eat and when and give them access to a greater variety. Your picky eater will be able to experiment with more foods that are better for them, and you may not have to struggle in order to get them to eat a healthy portion.

It also is easier for cats to eat and digest. Even though most of our cats are lazy housecats that would rather lay in a sunbeam than chase prey, their teeth are made to eat through flesh and chew thoroughly. Kibble and even soft food on the market simply don't offer that experience.

The Types of Diets You Should Know About

There are two main types of cat diets when it comes to making their food, and they are both fairly straightforward. Raw and cooked.

Raw food for your cats is probably the easiest and most straightforward. Because nothing is cooked and lost, you don't have to supplement it quite as much as cooked food – though it will still need some additives to make the whole meal balanced.

The biggest concern most people have with feeding their feline raw food is the potential bacteria, not just as they're eating it but in their stool when you clean it up. An upside, though, is that the stomach acid of a cat is about ten times more concentrated than a human's, which is already pretty great at breaking things down. For the most part, bacteria concerns aren't a problem. As long as the food has been handled and stored properly, you and your cat are safe.

Cooked food is an option for those who are worried about bacteria or too squeamish about offering up their pet a bowl of raw meat. I get it; it's not for everyone! The biggest downside to cooked food is that you need to add more supplements to their meals in order to create a balanced diet.

There is a middle ground, too. Sometimes called semi-cooked food, these recipes are generally baked briefly to kill any surface bacteria or pathogens. The interior remains raw. While this seems like it would be a 'best of both worlds' situation, it's important to note that you don't always know how much of the nutrients are removed or altered during this cooking process, so supplementing and providing a balanced diet can be harder.

THE RISKS: THEY EXIST

I would be doing you and your pet a great disservice if I wasn't honest with you in this section of the book. The truth of the matter is that I have helped countless people transition their own pets to a homemade diet, and it is not for everyone.

There are risks, there are safety concerns, and some people or cats simply can't handle it.

Before you jump right in, let's briefly talk about the risks involved with making your own cat food. This way, you will be completely informed and prepared moving forward and hopefully get the best experience possible.

Nutrition Issues

A later chapter will dive into exactly what this means, but nutrition is very serious and should be handled carefully. In the recipes portion of this book, I have many recipes detailing options using a cat-specific multivitamin and creating your own vitamin concoctions, depending on the recipe and what it might be missing.

It's incredibly important that you take your cat's nutrition seriously and take the right steps to meet all of their needs. Otherwise, they could get very sick.

Preexisting Medical Conditions

Most cats won't have this problem, but if your cat has a chronic underlying condition, you may want to reconsider making their food. Cats with kidney disease, for example, often experience dehydration more severely and cannot process their foods as well. They may need a special prescription diet.

In situations where you're not sure about your cat's health, I encourage you to talk to your vet. If they are on a medicated diet, ask why and if it is something you could replicate in your own kitchen or if it is too precise to do so. In all my years of helping others transition to homemade foods, I have only run into a few cats where medical issues prevented them from being able to transition to a homemade diet.

That said, it does happen. If your cat is sick or has issues, talk to your vet first. If your cat develops issues during the transition, slow down your transition and talk to your vet!

The Time

The biggest everyday 'drag' of making your cat's food is the time. Does this sound lazy of me? Maybe, but it's true!

Think about the time you spend right now feeding your kitty. Probably three minutes at the most, with washing up, right?

Scooping food into a bowl isn't exactly difficult, and scraping wet food is almost as easy.

Making food, though, takes time. It takes planning. It takes thought and effort, and honestly? It takes work. Even if you bulk prepare a few months at a time as we do in our household, those are big prep days. It's a lot easier overall to simply purchase food from the store and scoop it into your cat's food bowl.

Is it worth the time and the work? For our family and me, it is. I value my cat's health and happiness over the amount of time I put into the process.

I can't answer that question for you or your family, though – no one but you can really answer that question, after all. If you go into this process not thinking about the purchasing of individual ingredients, cutting, grinding, mixing, and portioning, though, you're going to be shocked the first time you make food and realize the work behind it.

To be clear, there is no shame if you decide this isn't for you. If you do not have the time or the energy, mental or physical, to make food, that is okay! Everyone has a different journey.

The Money

Addressed in other parts of this book, making your cat homemade food generally is more expensive than grabbing a big bag of Friskies from the pet store. Using whole, real ingredients is almost always going to be more expensive than going with a processed food product.

For some, this extra cost isn't feasible. Don't feel bad if you are living paycheck to paycheck and simply can't afford to switch from the cheapest brand you have always used. If you are concerned about the extra expenses, I would encourage you to figure out how much money on treats and food you're spending each month and calculate how much, based on sale prices in your local food ad, you would be increasing your cat's food budget too.

Compare the numbers and consider if this is something financially you want to do, can do, and are willing to do in the future.

Stigma

This is a bit of an odd one, but there is a big stigma against making your own cat food in many circles. For most people, this might never even come up, but for some, it is at least an annoyance.

A lot of folks don't understand cat food or cat nutrition, and they think you have to use a prepackaged, pre-weighed mixture to keep your cat healthy. You and I, of course, know that is not true, and you can give your cat the proper nutrition by cooking at home.

Once you start making your cat's food and start seeing the benefits, often we become sort of ambassadors for the role, sharing how much it has helped our pets and the difference. This is how I started helping so many other people to make their own Kitty Meal Plan – by becoming a cat food ambassador and sharing my experience with other owners.

You don't have to help people as I do, but you will probably face some backlash and misunderstandings from people who don't know what they are talking about. It's a small annoyance, but it does add up. No one likes to be judged!

No Going Back

That is a little intense, but the sentiment is the same. Once you start feeding your cats a raw food diet, you are 'stuck' with it. If, at some point, you become unable to continue their diet and want to transition back to commercial food, it's a long process of readjusting their body and their digestion to the food products. It can be a real hassle and, for many cats, a struggle. After eating 'good' for so long, going back to hard, crunchy, flavorless food isn't ideal.

When you make the decision to start making your cat's food, be sure it's something you could see yourself doing not just in six months but in six years. Just because you have a bit of time "right now" to do this doesn't mean you will in a few months or a year, so try to plan accordingly and be responsible.

Risks Associated

When done properly, with a vet's guidance at first to ensure your cat is properly healthy, there are few real 'risks' associated with feeding your cat a homemade diet. When done improperly, though, risks start popping up.

The biggest mistake I see people making is not handling and storing meats properly. Just because it's your pet's food doesn't mean it shouldn't be valued! Raw food should only be in the fridge for a few days, and you can freeze portions for later consumption if you make a larger batch. It's not hard! I freeze portions flat in a zip-top, freezer-safe bag, and they stack neatly and nicely in the freezer.

On top of that, be sure to treat the raw meat with respect. The chicken is going to your cat, but that doesn't mean you don't need to be careful about cross-contamination, cleaning your kitchen and work areas, and generally avoiding salmonella.

When feeding your cat food, the biggest risk I find is that cats are messy. Just because their digestion can handle raw chicken doesn't mean my carpets can, so there is a serious risk of cross-contamination and bacteria where they eat.

Providing your cats an easy to sanitize spot for their food consumption is important. Always thoroughly washing their bowl after eating and keeping their area very clean are two important steps to help prevent bacteria growth.

This is even more important if you have children in the house, even only visiting. How often do I touch my carpet and then lick my hand? Let's be honest, almost never. However, kids have no sense of self-preservation and put everything in their mouths. If you can't properly clean the area where your cats eat, any kids in the area can and will get sick.

Do The Risks Outweigh the Benefit?

Only you can decide. Before you make that choice, I encourage you to continue reading and thinking about it. Look at your lifestyle, the health of your cat or cats, and the time and money you have to dedicate to them.

For many people, the benefits far outweigh the risks and issues associated with homemade food.

TOOLS OF THE TRADE AND PREPPING TIPS

Stop! Before you go on and start these recipes, you're probably going to need some kitchen equipment to be able to prepare everything properly.

Kitchen Equipment

For some, this kitchen equipment may be standard. For most, though, you will have to get at least a few things. These are the tools that I highly recommend you own or invest in before you start making your own cat food. Some are essential, while others will just make your journey a whole lot easier.

Butcher's Knife

A good quality, sharp knife is going to be absolutely essential for this process. You're going to be breaking down a lot of meat, whether you're going raw or cooked, so it is important that you have something that is comfortable and durable.

You don't have to spend a ton of money on this item, but look for a knife that is a full tang at the very least. That means the metal of the blade extends all the way down through the handle. It's going to be much more reliable, last longer, and is less likely to snap or break when you're struggling through a bone or piece of thick meat.

A butcher's knife, or a cleaver, is different from a chef's knife. A chef's knife should never break through bones, just joints. There is a good chance that if you just do casual cooking in your kitchen, you will have to purchase a sturdy enough knife to really get through the meat, tissue, and bones.

Chef's Knife

You're going to want one of these as well. There are many different styles on the market right now at a variety of price points. Just like with a butcher's knife, you don't need to spend a lot of money. Just get something that is sturdy, a full tang, and that you like holding.

Knife Sharpener

This is actually a fairly important tool in your kitchen, so if you don't have one, it's time to invest. Get something that can keep all your knives nice and sharp, so you don't ever struggle to cut through ingredients.

Large Cutting Board

There is a good chance you are going to be cutting a lot of meat for your cat. It's just a fact! For the longest time, I used a small cutting board for all of my cat food prep, and it was annoying to have to shuffle pieces off to another board or plate and spill them off onto the counters.

My prep has gone faster and easier since getting a large board. I got the biggest cutting board that would reasonably fit into my dishwasher, but if you hand wash, I recommend the largest board that will fit in your sink. If you can't get it clean, it's not a very good investment. The extra working surface makes the whole process a lot easier.

On that note, though, I would avoid investing in a wood board. While these are beautiful, they can be difficult to keep clean when cutting a lot of raw products. You don't want any bacteria hiding in the wood grain, after all. I use a sturdy, restaurant-grade plastic cutting board I picked up from a local restaurant supply store. It is made to stand up to a lot of abuse, and when it becomes too nicked and damaged to reasonably keep clean, it will simply get replaced.

Meat Grinder

Perhaps the most important tool in your kitchen if you will be feeding a raw food diet is a quality meat grinder. The plastic attachment for the KitchenAid mixer isn't going to cut it here (trust me, I started with it).

A higher-quality meat grinder is going to do something that a cheap one can't, and that is grind through the bones. Bones are going to provide a ton of nutrients to your cat and make a huge difference in the quality of food they get.

While you can buy pre-ground meats from the butcher, I only recommend this method if you are going to be cooking their food. There are a few different reasons.

The biggest one is sanitation standards. When you're handling a whole chunk of raw meat, like a steak or a roast, the surface area is fairly limited. When that meat is ground, the surface area increases by a lot, and there is more room for bacteria to hide out in. Generally, standards for ground meats are lower in butchers because they know you're going to cook it before consuming it. This isn't a knock on your butcher, just a fact of life. By grinding your own meats, you have more control over the cleanliness of the meat and the equipment, a huge deal when feeding raw.

From a practical standpoint, I recommend a meat grinder that is easy to take apart and fits in your dishwasher. Hand washing every single piece gets old very fast.

You can get a quality meat grinder from a number of supply stores online. Read reviews, and look for something that can handle small bones. You also may be able to find some at restaurant auctions or even restaurant supply stores!

Optional: High Powered Blender or Food Processor

If you're not going to the meat grinder route but still want to feed raw, you can use a high-powered blender or food processor instead. When I say "high powered," I mean one of the expensive Vitamix blenders or something equally as impressive. The standard blender most of us have in the kitchen simply won't cut it, and you can easily burn the engine out with the bones.

Mixing Bowls

This should be obvious, but a set of mixing bowls for easy prep and organization will make the food process a lot easier.

Freezer Space

Not strictly essential, but very helpful. Having extra freezer space will let you prepare meals ahead of time and freeze the extra. This means you aren't preparing meals every single day for your cat but just pulling them out of the freezer the night before. I do a big prep a few times a year, but your space and their diet will dictate how you handle it.

Prep Containers

This is going to be different depending on how you are preparing and storing the food you make for your cats, but you're going to want something to keep it in if you will be doing it in batches, even small ones.

There are a variety of containers on the market. You can buy cat-specific plastic locking containers, glass containers, or even just use zip-top freezer bags.

If you are going to be bulk preparing and freezing your cat food, be sure that you get something rated for storage in the freezer. It should be air-tight with a great seal. I actually like using a vacuum sealer to get an airtight seal and keep the food fresher for longer, but I have used glass and plastic containers in the past without issue.

I label all of my containers with what they contain and when I made them. This keeps everything much more organized, allows me to have a first in, first out system (so nothing is hiding in my freezer for months at a time), and I always know what I'm grabbing. That way, the cats won't be eating the same exact meal 5 days in a row.

Label Maker

Speaking of labels – get a label maker! It's an extra expense, but it makes labeling everything so much easier, and I find it's great for many things in the kitchen. If you are using primarily zip-top bags, just a marker is enough, but you will want something like a label for anything reusable. For a long time, I simply used tape and a marker and would remove the tape when the container was empty. Not elegant, but it worked!

Kitchen Scale

A halfway decent kitchen scale is fairly important here because it's important that you get your portions of cat food correct. Eyeballing 2-3 ounces of something almost always ends in disaster. These are not expensive, and honestly? Useful for the kitchen all around, not just when prepping cat food.

Poultry Shears

Not strictly necessary, poultry shears are nice to have for cutting through more brittle bones, like chicken, and breaking up large pieces of meat into smaller chunks.

What You Should Know First

Before you jump into making your first batch, there are a few standard kitchen tips you should always follow. This is going to ensure the best quality food comes out of your kitchen for your cat and a safe, healthy final product.

Work Clean

You would think this goes without saying, but it's very important that you keep your kitchen and all the tools you are using to process your cat's food clean while you're cooking and prepping. This means sanitizing everything before use and cleaning thoroughly afterward, not just a light rinse. Handling raw meat comes with a lot of risks inherently, and you don't want to make yourself or your family sick. This includes your cat!

Follow Basic Food Safety

On the heels of work clean, follow all basic food safety guidelines. This means that you shouldn't let raw meats sit in the fridge for weeks at a time before consuming them; they should never be left out on the counter unnecessarily, and everything should be stored well.

The fact of the matter is, if you wouldn't consume it, you shouldn't ask your cat to consume it. There's no need to get pedantic about this – of course, I wouldn't eat chicken bones. But the sentiment of the statement remains true.

Size Matters

Think critically of the food you are feeding your cat. If you are grinding and using bones in their meals, you need to consider the size of the bones. Large bones can easily get stuck in their throat or mouth, causing them to choke, and even larger shards can get lodged in their digestive tract. When you are unsure about a size, go smaller.

THE METHOD, AND MEATS, THE MATTER

There are several different ways to feed your cat homemade food, even among the raw and cooked diets. I'm going to briefly break down your options here so you understand all of the choices you and your pet have for dinner. Ultimately, there isn't really a 'wrong' and 'right' choice among these, though obviously, there are wrong and right ways to go about it.

Choose what makes you comfortable and what your pet will like to eat. It's okay if you try one method and have to switch because they can't adjust, or you don't enjoy the prep at all. I won't judge.

Raw Methods

There are three main 'methods' of feeding your cat raw food. Grinding, *frankenprey*, and whole prey. As a note, all of these methods follow pretty much the same guidelines of 80/10/5/5. That is, 80-85% raw meat, 5-10% organ meat, and 5-10% raw, edible bones. T

Grinding is, by far, the most popular and common method for a number of reasons. For one, it's the easiest to manage in the long term for most people. It's also just a lot easier to look at and do. Some people can't get over the idea of seeing their beloved family pet munch on a whole piece of raw meat.

The benefits of grinding are that you can grind everything together with a meat grinder, bones and all, and the cat can easily consume everything without getting too picky. If your cat is transitioning from wet commercial food to a raw food diet, grinding is going to be the closest texture-wise, which may make it easier for them to adjust to, especially at first.

"Frankenprey" is a relatively new idea in the cat food community, but I have noticed it appealing to a lot more folks in recent years. The goal of frankenprey is to approximate what a cat's diet would be like in the wild – that is, they don't need to get 100% of their daily intake of anything each and every day. Instead, the diet offers them variety. As a whole, over the course of the week, the cat is consuming everything they need, but one day it may be more meat, while another has more fat or organs.

Frankenprey also generally follows a more whole approach, which is to say the food is not finely ground. Instead, proponents of the diet say that eating whole chunks of meat and bone engages the cat mentally and physically more, leading to greater health overall. The act of chewing, ripping, and tearing larger chunks of meat is also great for their dental health and helps keep teeth plaque-free.

While there is more freedom in a frankenprey diet, it's important to plan ahead more, too. You need to make sure that the overview of the meals is balanced and appropriate, even if, for dinner, your cat is only eating meat and no bones or organs. If you go the frankenprey route, I recommend planning out each week's meals in advance and knowing exactly what your cat will be eating. That will let you ensure your pet is getting everything they need, nutrition-wise, over the course of a day or a week.

Whole prey is… well, exactly how it sounds. Instead of piecing out the parts you want your cat to eat for that day, you provide them with a whole animal to work on. This could be mice, rats, young chickens, and more. Many of the benefits of frankenprey are transferred to the whole prey diet, including the act of eating a large piece of meat and flesh to help keep teeth clean and healthy.

The biggest downside of the whole prey diet is that your pet is eating a whole animal. For many owners, this is a step farther than they are willing to go, which I completely understand. I have fed both cats homemade food for a long time, but emotionally I cannot get over the image of my babies carrying dead animals around the house.

For cats transitioning from a traditional, commercial diet, they may struggle to identify a whole rodent or chick as food, which can lead to a lack of nutrition at first.

Cooked Methods

There are many reasons that you might choose cooked food over raw food. For some, just the idea of feeding their pets raw food can make them a little uncomfortable. In addition, there are an awful lot of people that don't recommend raw food for pets no matter what. I don't necessarily agree with these concerns, but everyone needs to consider their own comfort.

When you cook something, you fundamentally alter that item. By cooking the meat before you serve it to your cat, you are altering the nutritional content fundamentally. In order to meet all of your cat's dietary needs, you generally end up having to replace the nutrition you have lost in the form of supplements and additives. It is just a little bit trickier overall.

A Meat Breakdown

Picking the type of meat is almost as important as choosing to make the food itself! There are a whole host of meats on the market that your kitty is going to love. Determining what is right based on your budget, availability, and your cat's palette isn't easy, but it comes with time.

As an aside, I'm not recommending any one of these meats over another. In fact, I would encourage anyone making their own cat's food to shake it up and offer variety. Not only will that keep your cat interested in eating and make them happier (would you want to eat the same exact meal day in and day out?!), but some studies have suggested it can help prevent food intolerances. Only feeding chicken may mean their body will struggle with beef once they do eat it.

The best and most complete proteins to choose from include turkey, lamb, beef, chicken, and pork – all of the things you can easily find in grocery stores or butcher shops near you. But some of the more 'oddball' meat choices like venison, bison, goat, rabbit, and even pheasant are also complete proteins that your cats will enjoy. Unless you live in a very diverse area or have access to a rural butcher, these proteins are a lot harder to find. Ordering online is an option if you have your heart set on this sort of variety, though!

When it comes to organ meat, to get the most nutritional bang for your buck, I recommend liver and kidneys. Heart is also beneficial, but in my experience, it can be harder to find and more expensive. Remember that you don't have to 'match' the organs and the meat, too – if you can only find, say, beef heart and chicken liver, you can pair that with turkey meat, and everyone will still be happy and healthy.

As for the bones, there are a variety of options. You can choose to feed your cat meats that naturally have smaller, digestible bones, like quail or Cornish hens, or more commercially available options like chicken wings and backs. I recommend cutting them into smaller pieces with your butcher's knife or a sharp pair of shears before offering them.

You can offer up larger pieces of bone, but you should either break them up with a mallet or grind them down before serving. This gives your cat the best chance of eating and digesting them. Your cat will not be able to manage with a huge piece of bone, even with meat attached to it; they just don't have the jaw strength! One thing to consider is fish. You may have noted that I haven't mentioned fish at all when it comes to complete proteins your cat should eat. Most fish are a source of complete protein, and they do have a lot of health benefits for your cat, including a ton of healthy fatty acids.

However, they also have a lot of concerns. Because it's difficult to determine what toxins or heavy metals are in your fish, I recommend only using fish as a protein source if it is wild-caught and from a reputable source. Humans are much larger, so filtering out toxins from a piece of fish is easy. However, with cats, it can be a lot more of a struggle.

If you choose to feed fish as a regular part of their diet, be smart about it. Personally, I only supplement my cat's diet with fish as treats or a special occasion and do not rely on it as a complete, regular food source.

What You Should Avoid

Not all foods should go into your cat's food, and some are downright dangerous. When you're making your cat's food, it is only natural to want to add in extra flavor or 'fun' things to spice up their experience, but not everything should go in.

Most people know this, but chocolate is very dangerous for your cat. Truly, anything with caffeine should be avoided. Dark, milk, or white, it doesn't matter – it's not a healthy ingredient for them, so be sure to skip it.

One surprising no-go is grapes, or anything with grape juice or grape flavored. This includes raisins! Studies are questionable on what exactly makes this so toxic to animals, but grapes will seriously harm both dogs and cats in your household.

Riding on the back of grapes, alcohol should also be avoided. Housepets, in general, cannot metabolize alcohol properly, and it can do serious damage to their bodies in the long run.

Most adult cats cannot process dairy, no matter how much they may enjoy drinking it. While small doses of dairy probably won't hurt them, it can cause stomach distress and unpleasant bathroom experiences. There are a few exceptions to the dairy rule, which I go into in a recipe, but cats won't benefit from drinking a glass of milk. It should never be added to a regular part of a diet.

Both garlic and onion should be avoided. As much as we might love garlic, it's not at all good for a cat's digestion. Skip the 'extra' flavors!

Coconut water or actual coconut flesh should be avoided. In some situations, coconut oil can be a beneficial source of fat in small quantities, but coconut water has far too much potassium for their little bodies to properly handle.

Finally, you should never, ever feed your cat anything with xylitol in it. For most of us, this will never come up, but I remind every pet owner who I discuss food with. Some don't realize it! Xylitol is an artificial sweetener that is found in a lot of things, including sugar-free gum and some low calorie/low sugar nut butters, with the latter being how many pets consume it.

It's incredibly dangerous for cats to consume and should never be added to their food. Any store-bought treats or prepackaged foods not labeled for pet consumption should be read to ensure they don't have this ingredient.

As far as meats are concerned, most of the meat that you probably consume on an average day is totally fine and even good for your cats. However, there are some less unusual meats that are actually not a great idea.

Most wild game like boar, pig, and bear should be avoided for a number of reasons. Most of which is that you don't know what that animal consumed previously, and you don't know what parasites or toxins are hiding in them. Wild game like this can also transmit pseudorabies, which is a virus you want to avoid at all costs. For many of us, this isn't an issue (I've certainly never had the chance to cook with wild boar!), but it's something to keep in mind.

Most ocean fish also aren't a good primary source of protein. I know what you're thinking, my cat loves fish! And they probably do. However, most ocean fish is heavily contaminated with both toxins and heavy metals. As a sometimes treat, ocean fish is okay in small quantities but should never be fed primarily.

NUTRIENT BREAKDOWN FOR HEALTHY LIVING

The number one concern with homemade cat food is the nutrient content. It is vitally important for the health and safety of your cat that you craft their food with all the nutrients they need in a day for healthy living. This is a huge barrier for many people! It can be intimidating, and it is a lot easier just to pick up a bag with everything already in.

Cats are something called obligate carnivores or hypercarnivores. This means that they are a type of animal whose diet should be at least 70% meat, and their bodies do not properly break down and digest vegetation or greens to extract significant nutrients.

What does this mean?

It means your cat needs meat primarily in their diet! They simply can't handle a diet of vegetation or fruit because their bodies don't know what to do with it. This is why nearly every vet out there will never recommend a vegetarian or vegan diet for a cat, and all of the quality recipes for cat food are primarily meat.

There are three macronutrients that you need to consider when you are creating your cat's food and meals: protein, fat, and carbohydrates.

Protein is going to be the bulk of the diet. Made up of amino acids, protein is absolutely the most important part of your cat's diet. Protein is how your cat gets their energy, and it is essential for most of its bodily functions.

If you are thinking that you can get protein from sources other than meat, you're technically not wrong, but it's not exactly relevant. The reason is your cats need a complete protein source. Cats need 11 essential amino acids in their diet to function, as their body cannot produce them.

These eleven essential acids are Argentine, histidine, isoleucine, leucine, lysine, methionine, phenylalanine, taurine, threonine, tryptophan, and valine. Your cat requires these essential amino acids to function and thrive.

The vast majority of animal proteins, including fish, poultry, meat, and eggs, are considered complete proteins and contain all of these acids. With a complete protein source in their diet, your cat will have all the amino acids they need to function.

Fat is also essential in a balanced diet for your cat. Fats contain nutrients that will help move nutrients and energy around the body, as well as provide an extra, concentrated burst of energy after consumption. Just like with protein, fats can come from sources other than meat but will not be digested or utilized as well by your cat's body.

Your cat also cannot create the fatty acids they need by themselves. Just like with the amino acids in protein, they require this source. Without a proper fat source, most nutrients digested will not be able to be utilized – the most obvious outward sign will be a dull, rough coat. Cats with silky soft, vibrant coats often have the appropriate fat ratio in their diet!

Finally, we have carbohydrates. It is easy to see in commercially made cat food that carbohydrates are a central ingredient. The problem, however, is that a cat really cannot utilize or digest carbs properly. Because they are hypercarnivores, pretty much all of their diet should consist of fat and protein from animals. Corn, rice, pasta, and wheat are not on the menu in the wild, and their digestive systems can't really handle a lot of it.

A small amount of carbs in a cat's diet is recommended, generally, to help supplement energy and provide fiber. However, the amount of carbs that are in commercially produced foods are outrageously high and not recommended in the long term.

Now that you have seen the overview of your cat's dietary needs, the recommended ratios for standard homemade cat food are 50% protein, 40% fat, and 10% carbohydrates. The protein and fat should always be coming from an animal source, not a plant source.

An Additional Note on Carbs

10% is the maximum amount of carbohydrates your cat should be consuming. Ideally, you want to keep that number around 5-6%, and it should always be a complex carb. This includes oats, sweet potatoes, barley, and even chickpeas.

Unlike meat, these carbohydrates should be precooked. This will make them a lot easier for your cat's stomach to break down and digest, so they can actually use some of the nutrients.

Always avoid low-quality by-products for your carbohydrate additives, as they will provide no substance to the diet and just act as a filler. Making your own food allows you to avoid those kinds of fillers!

The Vitamins That Matter

Macronutrients are the wide view. Micronutrients, on the other hand, are the closer view. We're talking about small details here, which are important.

These are the nutrients your cats cannot create on their own, much like the amino acids in protein we talked about previously. That means they need to be supplemented in their diet.

Vitamin A = Vision, growth, immunity

Vitamin D = Bone structure and health

Vitamin E = Prevents and protects against aging and degeneration

Vitamin K = Helps clotting and bones

Vitamin B1 = Metabolisms both energy and carbs

Riboflavin = Helps enzymes

Vitamin B6 = Improves red blood cell function, the immune system, regulates hormones, and generations glucose

Niacin = Helps enzymes

Pantothenic acid = Helps the metabolism

Vitamin B12 = Helps enzymes

Folic acid = Helps break down amino acids

Vitamins aren't the only additive you need to consider as well. Minerals are just as important in your cat's diet! Essential minerals that need to be included in your cat's daily diet include

Calcium = Bone strength, muscle strength, nerve impulse

Phosphorus = Bone structure, energy, DNA structure

Magnesium = Hormone secretion, bone structure

Sodium = Nerve impulses

Potassium = Nerve impulses, enzyme reaction

Chlorine = Acid balance

Iron = Energy, blood production

Copper = Metabolism, blood cell and tissue formation

Zinc = Helps enzymes, healing, and skin function

Manganese = Bone structure helps enzymes and overall brain function

Selenium = Immune support

Iodine = Metabolic function

If this seems like a lot to keep track of, well, it can be! That's one of the downsides of making your own pet food, honestly. You need to be sure you are meeting all of their dietary needs, and that includes the extra vitamins and minerals they need. The good news is, in many foods or supplements, your cat will get multiple of these. You're not going to be adding 30 different things into your cat's food!

How to Access These Supplements

There's a good chance that depending on the methodology and processes you use, you're going to have to minimally supplement your cat's food. As mentioned before, you won't be adding 12 pills on top of their meat sources. However, in order to ensure they are healthy and eating a balanced diet, you're probably going to have to add some in.

So, where can you get these?

Many more comprehensive pet supply stores or even vet offices will have supplements for cats that should provide much of what their diet may be lacking. Think of them as the multivitamin of the cat world. You can simply top their food with it or mix it in.

Depending on what you are feeding them as well, you may only have to supplement a small bit. In that case, buying specific supplements, like just taurine or just vitamin E, is totally fine. These do not necessarily need to be pet-only supplements! You can pick them up online or at a local health food store.

Make sure they are of good quality, with no extra fillers, and are easy to use. That means they either come in a capsule that you can easily break open or, ideally, a powdered form you can sprinkle on top of the meat you are mixing. Liquids are okay, and your cat might not mind them, but I have found my cats can taste liquid vitamins and are not big fans. I made the mistake once of bulk buying a B-Complex liquid supplement, and it was not a fun time for anyone involved.

The Proper Caloric Intake

We all know the old '2,000 calories a day is standard' for humans… but what is the standard for cats? Obviously, they are smaller, so an awful lot less.

There are a number of factors that will change their required caloric intake, including age, sex, current weight, activity level, and even if they are altered (spayed or neutered).

When they are young, a 5-pound kitten will need about 200 calories a day. They're growing, and they need all the energy they can get!

If you're feeding a mom or a lactating or pregnant mother, they will also need extra calories. For your 10-pound pregnant or lactating cat, they will need about 600 calories a day. At 15 pounds, they will need about 850. 20 pounds will need upwards of 1,000 pounds. Remember that during nursing, your female cat will likely lose weight no matter how much she is eating. It's a lot of energy and effort to feed all her kittens!

For your average house cat living that good housecat life, their caloric intake is a lot smaller. At 5 pounds, a grown housecat should be getting about 170 calories a day. At 10 pounds, they need about 280. At 15, 360 calories, and at 20, it goes up to about 440 calories.

Note: This is the number of calories given here are to maintain a healthy weight and diet, but each cat and activity levels are different. Your cat could be 10 pounds and overweight or 15 pounds and underweight. It's important to adjust calories to get and keep your cat at a healthy weight.

For some pets, that will be to reduce their caloric intake until they reach a healthy weight. For others, that will be adding extra calories to bring them back up to a healthy weight. Once they hit their ideal weight, you can level out the calories one way or the other until everyone is happy and healthy.

If you're not sure if your pet is at a healthy weight or what a healthy weight would be for their size and bone structure, I recommend talking to your vet! They should be able to help quite a bit and potentially give you guidelines for the average caloric intake that is right for your cat.

Once you start feeding them and figuring out their eating habits and appetites, you should be able to settle on a healthy number of calories per day for their body type and weight. The first few weeks, or even a few months, of feeding, is all about adjusting and looking out for them. Don't fret if they gain a bit of weight or lose a bit of weight at first. You can easily balance it out, and they won't hate you because they were a little snacky one evening!

TIPS FOR THE TRANSITION

Before you jump into recipes and prepping all of your cat's meals, I'm going to take a brief pause to talk about the best way to transition your cats to this diet.

As a pet owner, you are probably aware cats can be notoriously picky. I've always joked it is because they remember when they were worshiped as gods in Egypt, but really, your cat just knows what they like and what they don't. Sometimes, it can take them a while to come around to something new.

There are two big things you need to consider here: the personal preferences of your cat and their digestive adjustment.

Getting Your Cat to Love Homemade Foods

Tastes are different for everyone, so it's going to be an adjustment for your cat no matter what they are used to eating.

However, it's going to be the biggest adjustment if your cat is used to eating commercial dry foods.

I've actually talked to a lot of pet owners about this, and the easiest way most have found to transition is to start them on a partially wet food diet. Get your cat used to eating a softer food texture from a can. Do this slowly, though – add a tablespoon or two of it to their food each day, and up the wet food while decreasing the dry each day.

When choosing wet food, I recommend getting high-quality food that is grain-free and made from whole ingredients, with no meal or byproducts. You want to start trading up the quality of their food, not making it worse!

If you really want to go further, you can check the fridge sections of your local pet store to see if they have premade cat food that will closely resemble what you are going to be making your cat. I find this food tends to be very overpriced for what it is, but for some picky cats, this might be necessary.

Ideally, you're going to make this transition within a week's time. A full 7 days is a good time frame to get your cat adjusted to this.

Once your cat has started eating and accepting the wet food, you can start their transition to homemade foods. If you have a very picky eater, I recommend starting with dehydrated food or treats. These are similar in texture to what your cat is used to eating – dry, crunchy food – but they don't have any extra ingredients, so it will taste like what you want them to eat.

Top their wet food with a few pieces of the dehydrated treats. Once they accept and enjoy that, start incorporating the actual homemade food into their bowl each day, a little at a time.

Again, this should be a long, low-stress process for everyone involved. Start with just a bit of the homemade food with their standard meal, and up the amount of homemade food each day while decreasing the wet or processed foods.

There are a few additional beginner's tips I can recommend when you get to this stage, based on my own experience and coaching others through this process.

First of all, I recommend starting with organ meat, like liver. This is naturally going to be very appealing to a cat, and it's got a lot of nutrients in it. If your cat will gobble down a few chunks of liver, this is a sign the transition should go fairly smoothly.

Secondly, I recommend warming the food before serving. Don't go in starting your poor on hunks of raw, cold food; this isn't going to appeal to them for a number of reasons. You don't want to cook it, of course, but by placing it in a plastic bag and letting it sit in a bowl of warm water for 15-20 minutes, you're really taking the chill off. This is going to make it a lot more palatable for your cat.

Even warm, if your cat is struggling, you don't have to call off the attempt yet. If your cat is leaving their homemade food and eating the canned food, try doing the same thing – sprinkling your dehydrated treats over the top of the food, or crumbling them into smaller bits first, so they have to eat some of the raw food to get to the dehydrated treats, too.

You can also try covering the new food with catnip, which might entice your cat enough to give it a few tastes and make them realize, hey, this is delicious food, too.

Finally, before all else fails, you can simply leave it. Give your cat a day or two to get hungry, and keep offering homemade food. At some point, there's a good chance they will break down and realize what you are doing and eat the food. This isn't cruel, and the typical housecat won't starve because they haven't eaten in a day, I promise. Sometimes a cat needs a little extra push to understand what you are offering them is, in fact, food – and yummy food, at that!

Be very aware of your cat's limitations and health, though!

Getting Your Cat's Body Adjusted to Homemade Food

The most important part of everything I outlined above is the time. Adjusting your cat to a new and very different diet should be a slow and steady change over the course of days, if not weeks.

Think about it this way: say you've only eaten fast food your entire life. Entire life, you swung by McDonald's on the way to work for breakfast, grabbed Taco Bell for lunch, and finished your day off with a gas station hot dog or a Wendy's burger.

None of it is good, healthy, or fresh, but it kept you going.

Now all of a sudden, you have fresh, healthy foods to eat every day. If you quit your fast food habit cold turkey and immediately changed to fresh foods, your body would be messed up for quite a while. Your stomach and organs would have no idea how to process it, and you would probably end up feeling sick to your stomach for a while before you were done adjusting.

The same thing is happening to your cat, especially if they are used to eating dried, commercially available food. It wasn't great for them, and the change to a healthy, nutritious diet is going to be a huge adjustment to their stomachs.

You want to ease your cat into any diet change, especially a major one like this. Do a slow addition to their diet over a long period of time, and be sure to monitor their health. If their bathroom habits or stool has major changes, especially for longer than a day, slow down your process and ease back into it.

Ultimately, you are making this change for the health of your cats. You don't want to potentially make them sick from something that is supposed to make them feel better!

Always Consult Your Vet

If you have done any research outside of this book on switching to homemade food for your cat, this advice might go against what you have seen. However, in my opinion, it can be incredibly dangerous to not talk to your vet.

Not all vets are going to be well versed in homemade foods, and not all will understand your desire to make your own cat food. Even considering that, having a vet on board to monitor your cat's nutrient levels at the beginning of the journey and to do regular checkups to ensure all of their levels are properly balanced.

If you are worried your vet won't take you seriously, come prepared. Print out the section of this book on nutrition. Take notes, bring recipes, and show your vet that you have done your research and you understand the importance of a balanced diet for your cat!

If your cat has any medical concerns or health issues, it is even more important to talk to your vet first. There are certain medical conditions that may be worsened by changing diets or increasing a specific vitamin or mineral, so you should be aware of what your specific cat needs before you go into it. Ultimately what matters most is the health of your cat!

If your vet does not agree with your decision or refuses to help you, I would consider switching vets to someone that will listen to you. There are many people who try homemade food for their pets and get it wrong without ever realizing their pet has complex food needs. You have made it this far in my book, though, so clearly, you are not one of them. Bring your newfound knowledge on nutrition and feeding to your appointment, and make it clear you want to do it right.

THE RECIPES

This is the section you have been really waiting for, the actual recipes.

In these, I'm going to recommend using a variety of supplements depending on the recipe and the portion size. You don't have the use the brands that I use, but I recommend you find something relatively equivalent that is available to you. Some recipes use a single multi-supplement that I can easily find in pet stores near me. Others utilize a variety of supplements.

This is for several reasons, but the biggest one is to give you variety. Maybe you can't find the multi-supplement formula I use? There are options. Maybe you don't want 12 different supplements just for your cat hanging out in a cabinet? There are options.

It's not one-size-fits-all, so be sure to keep that in mind as you are reading through the recipes. In no way am I sponsored or even affiliated with any of the products I'm using. I am simply a happy customer with two happy kitties.

It's important to always follow recipes and portions and consider your cat's size and caloric needs. If it seems like there is a lot that goes into your cat's healthy eating, that is because there is. However, it doesn't always feel so overwhelming.

Once you get a few recipes down you and your cat love, and you get used to their needs, it becomes much easier to manage in the long run. Soon, you'll be surprised you ever felt it was stressful!

In short? It's okay if you're overwhelmed at the moment. It will get easier.

CHICKEN RECIPES

Chicken is a complete protein, and I find most cats love it. Some struggle with the idea of salmonella, which I understand is a concern. However, cats have stomach acid far stronger than most animals, including our own. The risk of them getting sick from raw chicken is incredibly low, no higher than from any other meat you are feeding them. Realistically, no higher than any other food you are feeding them.

The one thing I will recommend, though, is to pay attention to how your cat eats. If your cat prefers to drag their food around the house before eating it, try resituating a bowl of food, so it is already at their preferred place. I mentioned this in a previous section, but it's good to remind you as well.

Obviously, you don't want raw or undercooked chicken being dragged through your carpet or across your house!

Chicken can come from any number of sources, including your local grocery store. If you can't find organ meat in the cases at the local meat market, grocer, or butcher, I recommend asking: there is a good chance if they don't have any on hand, they will happily order some for you or let you know when they get a restock.

I have had great luck with organ meats at local international markets as well, which seem to have the best, and freshest supply in my area.

Basic Ground Chicken

As simple as it gets, this is a great place to start if you're unsure of where you're going with this diet or how to start.

Ingredients

Approximately 6lbs of chicken breast and thigh, raw

7.5 ounces chicken livers

2 cups filtered water

40 grams of alnutrin with Calcium or another all-encompassing cat vitamin

Steps

1. Chop your chicken and livers into small to medium-sized pieces. Combine in a bowl, mixing well.

2. If grinding, freeze your meat for 15-20 minutes for best results before feeding it through a meat grinder.

3. In a small container, mix the water with the alnutrin until dissolved, then pour over your meat.

4. Mix well until the meat is coated with the liquid.

5. Portion into individual meals, label, and store.

Complex Chicken Meal

Ingredients

3-4 chicken thighs with drumsticks, raw, with the bones removed (about 4 pounds)

14 ounces chicken heart, raw

7 ounces chicken liver, raw

4 egg yolks

1.5 cups filtered water

2 tablespoons bone meal

1 teaspoon lite salt

200 mg taurine

800 IU vitamin E

200 mg vitamin B-complex

1 tablespoon psyllium husk for fiber

Steps

1. Cut your chicken and organ meats into small to medium-sized pieces. Add about half of the skin and fat attached to the chicken, but not all. Dark meat already has plenty of fat naturally.

2. If grinding, place your chicken and meats in the freezer for 20 minutes before grinding.

3. In a small bowl, mix your water, lite salt, all of your vitamins, and the psyllium husk. Stir together until everything is mixed.

4. Pour your vitamin and water mixture over your meat and mix well.

5. Portion and store until ready to consume.

Chicken and Veggies

A little more complex but still easy, this recipe goes over well with all the cats I've introduced it to. The eggs add both a creaminess and a richness to it, plus lots of nutrients.

Ingredients

4 pounds of chicken thighs, raw

5 ounces of chicken or turkey liver, raw

15 ounces of chicken or turkey hearts, raw

1 carrot, grated

½ cup frozen peas, thawed*

4 egg yolks

2 cups filtered water

40 grams of alnutrin with calcium

*If you use canned peas instead, be sure to buy a can with no sodium added, and rinse well.

Steps

1. Chop your chicken thighs, hearts, and livers into small to medium-sized pieces. Mix well in a bowl.

2. If grinding, freeze for 20 minutes before grinding meats together for best results.

3. In a steamer or in boiling water, cook the carrot and peas together into very soft. Remove and strain.

4. Add your egg yolks and steamed vegetables to your meat and organs mixture, and mix well.

5. In a small container, mix your water and alnutrin together until well combined. Pour over your meat, egg, and vegetable mix and combine one more time until everything is well incorporated.

6. Portion and store until ready to consume.

Chicken and (Extra) Veggies

Want even more vegetables? Some cats love them, and if your cats are one of them, this is a great recipe!

Ingredients

5 pounds boneless, skinless chicken meat

8 ounces chicken liver, raw

5 ounces grated carrot

6 ounces snow peas

2 cups water

40 grams alnutrin with calcium

Steps

1. Chop your chicken into small to medium-sized chunks. Place in a freezer for 15-20 minutes to firm up.

2. Grind your cold chicken breast through your grinder.

3. Chop up your chicken liver into relatively small pieces, and mix with the ground chicken.

4. Steam your carrot and snow pea until very soft, 6-7 minutes. Drain, dry, and add to your ground meats.

5. In a small container, mix your water and alnutrin until dissolved.

6. Pour your nutrient water on your meat and mix well.

7. Portion and store until ready to consume.

Semi-Cooked Chicken and Eggs

If you're interested in partially cooking your cat's food, this simple recipe is a great place to start.

Ingredients

3-4 pounds of chicken thighs, bones removed

4 ounces of chicken liver

2 tablespoons bone meal

2 soft boiled eggs*

1 cup filtered water

5000 mg salmon oil

400 IU vitamin E

75 mg vitamin B-complex

2000 IU taurine

1 teaspoon lite salt

*You should lightly cook the whites, but you can leave the yolks completely raw. Soft boiling is by far the easiest way to do this, but you can poach them if you prefer. Don't microwave the eggs, though, as they can explode in the microwave and lead to injury and burns.

If your cat refuses this meal, try taking the egg out. My cats love cooked eggs, but I have found not all do.

Steps

1. Preheat your oven to 350 degrees.

2. Lay out your chicken thighs and chicken liver on a baking tray. Bake, uncovered, for about 15 minutes. You aren't cooking the chicken all the way through in this situation, just about halfway! It may take as little as 10 minutes, or as much as 20, depending on how thick your thighs are.

3. Remove from the oven and immediately submerge in cold water to stop the cooking process. Alternatively, you can place the thighs in the freezer for 10-15 minutes if you have the space.

4. Once cooled, cut your chicken into small to medium-sized pieces. Add your cooked egg whites (not the yolks!).

5. In a separate bowl, add your egg yolks, water, bone meal, lite salt, and all of the supplements. Mix well.

6. Once well mixed, pour this over your meat mixture. Mix well.

7. Portion and store until ready to consume.

Boiled Chicken with Healthy Greens

This is one that I have confused both friends and family with because it smells genuinely delicious while cooking. It's relatively easy to put together and a favorite for cooked meals.

Ingredients

3 pounds roasting chicken, quartered

4 cups filtered water

2 celery stalks with leaves

1 cup finely chopped or grated carrot

½ bunch fresh parsley, chopped

½ cup uncooked barley

1 tablespoon Brewer's yeast

1 tablespoon fresh lemon juice

5 ounces frozen spinach, thawed, drained, and chopped finely

1 cup green beans, trimmed and chopped

½ teaspoon lite salt

Steps

1. In a stockpot or Dutch oven, place your chicken, water, and lite salt. Simmer for about an hour and a half, or until the chicken is very tender.

2. Remove from heat and strain your chicken broth into a bowl. Place the broth in the fridge or freezer until chilled enough to have the top layer of fat solidify.

3. Meanwhile, remove the meat from the bones and chop it into bite-sized pieces. Discard the bones, fat, and skin.

4. Once your broth is chilled, skim that top layer of excess fat. Don't worry; the broth is plenty rich without it.

5. Add your skimmed broth to a pot along with the celery, chopped carrots, brewer's yeast, lemon juice, and barley. Cover and let simmer for 20 minutes.

6. At the 20-minute mark, add in your green beans, chopped spinach, and chicken. Continue to cook for another 15-20 minutes, or until the beans are soft.

7. Let cool before portioning and storing until served.

Small Serving Chicken and Vegetables

If you only want to prep a small amount of cooked food – maybe a day or two's worth of food – this is a great recipe for you. I use frozen bagged vegetables and over steam them, so they are nice and soft, but you can buy fresh and use a steamer if you prefer.

Ingredients

1 cup cooked chicken

¼ cup broccoli, steamed well

¼ cup carrots, steamed well

1-2 tablespoons of no sodium chicken broth, as needed

8 grams alnutrin with calcium

Steps

1. Using a fork, lightly mash your vegetables to start breaking them down, and ensure you don't have any hard chunks in the center.

2. Place the chicken, broccoli, carrots, and alnutrin in a food processor. Add 1 tablespoon of broth and blend until well mixed and very smooth but not soupy. If it doesn't come together, add a little more broth until blended well.

3. Serve immediately, or portion and store until ready to consume.

Easy Homemade Stock

Depending on where you live, you may struggle to find no-salt-added chicken stock for your cat's meals. Stock adds a ton of nutrients, as well as liquid, and it should be included in many meals. If you can't find a good one or don't want to pay extra for it, this recipe is incredibly easy to make. You can store it in the fridge or freezer.

I always make my stock in an Instant Pot, an electric pressure cooker. It takes less time and yields a better final product. However, you can easily make this on the stovetop, too.

Ingredients

2-3 pounds of chicken feet

3-4 liters of water

Steps, Stovetop

1. In a large stockpot, add your chicken feet and cover with water. Bring to a boil, and then reduce heat to simmer.

2. Let simmer, covered, for 4-5 hours, checking occasionally and adding water as needed if it gets too low.

3. Once you feel the chicken essence of the feet has fully incorporated, allow the stock to cool slightly before straining and storing.

Steps, Pressure Cooker

1. Place your chicken feet in your pressure cooker. Fill with water to the lower 'Max' line inside the pot.

2. Seal and pressure cook on high for 45 minutes.

3. Once finished, allow all pressure in the stock to release naturally. This can take anywhere from 30-40 minutes itself since there is so much stock. There is no rush!

4. When the internal pressure has come down, open the lid and strain the stock. Store until ready to use.

Recipe Notes

Can't find chicken feet? There are a few places you can find them. Ask your local butcher, as they may be able to source you some for cheap. My local international market also has chicken feet almost all the time, though I do have to ask the meat department occasionally.

If no one near you has them, feel free to substitute with 2-3 chicken legs, with the bone and skin attached.

Cat Chicken Soup

This recipe builds from our previous one, but you can use store-bought stock or broth instead if you prefer!

Ingredients

3-4 cups of homemade (or store-bought) no sodium chicken stock

1 cup cooked chicken

¼ cup diced chicken livers

¼ cup diced chicken hearts

1 carrot

1 stalk of celery

¼ cup brown rice

½ zucchini

½ cup frozen peas

Steps

1. Finely chop your carrot, celery, zucchini, and chicken. I use a mix of white and dark when I make this generally, but use what you have – just make sure it's prepared with cats in mind. (No toxic seasonings or salt)

2. In a medium pot, add everything but your peas. Bring to simmer.

3. Let cook for 10 minutes before adding all the vegetables except for the peas.

4. Continue cooking for 20-30 minutes, or until everything is very soft.

5. Add your peas, and cook an additional 5 minutes, or until heated through and cooked. Alternatively, you can use a can of peas with no salt, rinsed.

6. Let cool some before offering to your cat.

Recipe Note

Struggling with a cat who doesn't feel great or doesn't want to eat? This is a great recipe to use. Add 2-3 tablespoons of catnip in when you add your vegetables after the brown rice has started to cook. It should lend a green color to the soup, but your cat will certainly perk up at the chance to eat it.

BEEF RECIPES

For many, beef is the natural protein choice. However, beef on its own is a bit more complex since the bones aren't exactly easy to manage. Most recipes with beef also include chicken, so you can have a balanced diet.

As with chicken, beef can be purchased anywhere that you normally would buy your beef. If you are feeding raw, be sure to grind the beef yourself, not rely on a butcher or grocery store to grind it for you!

Beef and Organ Mix

This is generally a mix I make when I'm 'running out' of other ingredients, as it sort of has everything but the kitchen sink. However, it is incredibly nutritious, and my cats love it.

Ingredients

2 pounds of beef, raw

100 grams beef heart*

100 grams chicken hearts

100 grams chicken liver

2 egg yolks

2 tablespoons ground bone meal

¼ teaspoon lite salt

½ cup filtered water

2000 mg of taurine

2000 mg of salmon oil

400 IU of Vitamin E

200 mg of Vitamin B-complex

*Can't find beef heart? You can swap this out for an extra 100 grams of chicken hearts instead!

Steps

1. Cut your beef and organ meats into chunks. Place in a large bowl and freeze for at least 20 minutes.

2. Grind your meat mixture.

3. In a separate container, mix your eggs, bone meal, and water, along with lite salt and all the vitamin supplements.

4. Pour this over your ground beef and organ mixture, and combine.

5. Portion and store until ready to consume.

Beef Combo

Can't decide if your cat prefers beef or chicken more? Give them both!

Ingredients

2 pounds beef

1 pound chicken livers

1 pound chicken hearts

1 pound chicken wings

4 cans of tuna, packed in water

4 cans of sardines, packed in water

2000 mg of taurine

400 IU of Vitamin E

200 mg of Vitamin B-Complex

Steps

1. Chop your chicken wings and beef into small to medium-sized pieces. Place in the freezer for 15-20 minutes to firm up.

2. Grind roughly using your grinder.

3. Roughly chop your chicken hearts and livers. Add that to your ground meats, along with all your tuna and sardines, and all your vitamins

4. Mix thoroughly until everything comes together and the vitamins are well distributed.

5. Portion and store until ready to serve.

Meatloaf, But For Cats

This is a fun one! Who doesn't like meatloaf? Careful; coming out of the oven, it actually looks and smells like standard meatloaf... okay, a little fishier, but if someone in the household isn't paying attention, I can see the problem.

I use pre-ground beef from my local market for this recipe because it's being cooked, but you can grind your own if you prefer.

Ingredients

2 pounds 90/10 ground beef

2 pounds ground turkey, dark meat if possible

1 pound chicken liver

1 pound chicken heart

½ cup zucchini, grated

¼ cup mixed berries (frozen and thawed is fine!)

¼ cup broccoli, cut into very small pieces or grated through a box grater

¼ cup kale

2 cans sardines, packed in water, drained

Steps

1. Preheat your oven to 350 degrees.

2. Place your kale, broccoli bits, berries, zucchini, and sardines in a food processor. Pulse until smooth. Place in a large bowl.

3. Add your chicken liver and hearts to the food processor, and pulse until it is the consistency of ground meats – it doesn't have to be a paste, but broken up is good. You can also put this through a grinder, though then you would have to clean the grinder after with little benefit.

4. Add your organ meats to the vegetable mix, along with both ground meats.

5. Mix well, using your hands to get everything together.

6. Transfer your meatloaf mixture to a large baking dish.

7. Bake, uncovered, for 50-60 minutes or until it reaches an internal temperature of at least 160 degrees.

8. Remove and let cool completely before portioning and storing.

Beef Soup

It's no secret cats love being warm, right? Well, soup is the perfect way to warm up a cat on a cold winter's day. One of my first apartment moves after getting Babs and DD was incredibly drafty in the winter, and I could tell they hated being cold. In addition to the usual ways to keep them warm and happy, I created this easy soup recipe for them. It's easy and delicious, perfect for any cat who wants to be warm and happy.

Ingredients

2-3 pounds of beef bones

3-4 liters of water

2 teaspoons apple cider vinegar

½ cup carrots, chopped small

½ cup frozen peas

½ cup green beans, chopped small

Steps

1. In a stockpot or large Dutch oven, add your beef bones, apple cider vinegar, and cover with water.

2. Bring to a simmer, then add your carrots and peas.

3. Let simmer until the meat has fallen off of the bones and the vegetables are very tender.

4. Strain carefully, reserving the stock.

5. Put the stock back into the pot, and add the bones with the meat removed. Set the meat and vegetables to the side.

6. Bring back to a simmer and continue to cook, stirring occasionally, for 10-20 hours, or as long as you can essentially.

7. Once cooking time is done, skim any fat from the top, add the peas to allow to cook until soft (usually 5-10 minutes), and then

return veggies and meat to the broth.

8. Portion and store until ready to consume.

TURKEY RECIPES

Turkey is a great alternative to chicken and offers a lot of benefits. It's also often cheaper than chicken, especially around the holidays. I usually stock up on a few frozen birds after Thanksgiving, when even the high-quality locally raised birds are inexpensive.

I have found, however, turkey organs are far less common. You can easily substitute chicken organs instead if that is all you can find.

In general, I mostly feed my cats the dark meat of the turkey. It's fattier, which is good, and more nutritionally dense.

The Holiday Special

Pumpkin is fantastic for a pet's digestive tract, and this recipe makes full use of it. With the pumpkin and the turkey, it really feels like your cat is included in the holiday celebrations.

Ingredients

6 pounds dark meat turkey, raw

7 ounces chicken or turkey liver, raw

2 cups filtered water

2 cups organic, all-natural pumpkin puree*

40 grams alnutrin with calcium

*It's important to read the label before you pick up pumpkin puree! You want just the puree, which is simply cooked pumpkin blended. You don't want the 'pie mix' or 'pie filling,' which can have sugar and spices added to it. You can also easily make this yourself by roasting off a pumpkin, scooping the flesh from the skin, and blending it.

Instructions

1. Cut your turkey and liver into small to medium-sized chunks and place in a large bowl. You can add some of the skin, but don't include all of it – that's a lot of extra fat, especially with dark meat.

2. In a medium bowl, mix your alnutrin and water together until mixed. Add your pumpkin, and mix again.

3. Pour over your turkey and chicken liver and mix well until everything is incorporated and coated in pumpkin.

4. Portion and store until ready to consume.

Turkey and Rabbit Surprise

It's not often we can get rabbit in my area, but when we do, I like to stretch it as far as I can. That includes using this recipe, which mixes rabbit and turkey. It also utilizes the rabbit bones for extra calcium. If you wish, you can sub the bones for bone meal.

Ingredients

2.5 pounds of fresh turkey breast, raw

2 pounds fresh rabbit, raw

14 ounces chicken hearts, raw

7 ounces chicken liver, raw

2 cups water

4 egg yolks

1 teaspoon lite salt

4,000 mg salmon oil

800 IU Vitamin E

200 mg Vitamin B-complex

1 tablespoon psyllium husk powder for fiber

Steps

1. Using a sharp knife, cut your turkey and rabbit into small to medium-sized pieces, removing and reserving the bones from both. You should remove most of the fat and skin from the turkey but leave the skin on the rabbit.

2. Cut your liver and hearts into smaller chunks, and add them to a bowl with your bones. Place everything in the freezer for 20 minutes.

3. Process your bones and your organ meat through the grinder.

4. Mix this with your turkey and rabbit portions.

5. In another bowl, add your egg yolks, vitamins, lite salt, and water. Mix well, and then pour over your meat and bones.

6. Mix once more.

7. Portion and store until ready to consume.

Turkey Pasta

Similar to another recipe in this book with salmon, this is a fun treat meal on occasion. It actually makes a creamy, delicious final product, so says my cats. This is full of vitamins and good fats and is an excellent choice for a kitty with an upset stomach or a picky eater.

Ingredients

1 pound ground turkey, lean

1 cup small pasta, whole grain

2 egg whites

½ cup plain nonfat Greek yogurt

½ teaspoon bone meal

100 mg taurine

½ teaspoon catnip

Steps

1. Add your turkey to a nonstick skillet over medium heat. Cook, breaking up the turkey until everything is browned.

2. Drain excess fat and remove the turkey. Set aside.

3. Place the skillet back on the heat and cook your egg whites lightly until set.

4. Meanwhile, in a medium skillet, bring water to boil and cook your pasta according to the package, usually about 10 minutes. Drain when finished.

5. In the bowl of a food processor, add your cooked pasta, turkey, egg, yogurt, bone meal, catnip, and taurine. Pulse until well combined and chopped thoroughly. It does not have to be a paste.

6. Allow to cool to room temperature before serving.

RABBIT RECIPES

We don't get rabbit a lot in my area, but when local butchers have it on special (usually around the holiday times), I will pick them up for my cats. It's something different and certainly a more unique protein.

Rabbit is generally leaner and gamier, so it may not be to taste for every cat.

Easy Rabbit Dinner

This is a great recipe when you're really not feeling like putting in a whole lot of work, but your babies still need food. Because it uses the whole animal, bones and organs included, you don't need a whole lot extra.

Ingredients

8 pounds rabbit, raw and whole*

2 cups filtered water

35 grams of alnutrin meat and bone supplement

*For this recipe, you want as much of the rabbit as you can get, including the organs and bones. The heart and liver are both essential. If you, for some reason, cannot add 200 grams of chicken or turkey hearts and 100 grams of chicken liver while reducing the rabbit weight included by about 300 grams.

Steps

1. Cut your rabbit into medium-sized chunks. Leave the skin and bones intact. Freeze for 20 minutes.

2. Grind your rabbit, bones and all.

3. In a small bowl, mix your water with the alnutrin. Pour over your meat and bone mixture.

4. Mix well.

5. Portion and store until ready to consume.

Cooked Rabbit Stew

This tends to be a lot of work for the amount of food it makes, but if you want to serve cooked rabbit instead of raw, it's a good option. It also scales up well, so you can easily double the recipe for many meals.

Ingredients

1 pound of rabbit meat

1 teaspoon olive oil

¼ teaspoon of parsley

¼ teaspoon of thyme

¼ teaspoon marjoram

¼ teaspoon rosemary

¼ teaspoon lite salt

10 grams sweet potato

10 grams carrot

10 grams celery stalk

10 grams peas

1-2 cups no-sodium vegetable stock

Steps

1. In a small to medium Dutch oven, add your olive oil and heat over medium to medium-high.

2. Add your rabbit and cook for 3-4 minutes on each side, or until you develop a lovely golden color.

3. Once browned, add your stock, along with all your seasonings. Scrape the bottom to get all the brown bits off.

4. Reduce heat to medium-low and cook, stirring occasionally, for 20 minutes.

5. While cooking, chop your vegetables into small pieces.

6. Once 20 minutes is up, add your vegetables and check the broth levels. You may need to add a little bit more, so it does not get too dry.

7. Continue cooking for 30-40 minutes, or until the rabbit is able to shred easily.

8. Cool to room temperature before serving or portion and store until ready to consume. You can also put this through a food processor for cats who struggle with chunks of meats and vegetables.

FISH RECIPES

Most fish are fine as a "sometimes" meal. While they should never be your cat's only source of protein (unless they have severe allergies, in which case I recommend talking to your vet!), cats really do love a good fish meal.

I like to cycle through a handful of these fish meals to keep things interesting, and my cats enjoy them greatly.

Blended Trout

'Blended' is a strong word, but it's a little better than 'trout smoothie.' I like using this as a topping for special occasions or when my cats have been having a hard time. It can, however, be a full meal occasionally.

Ingredients

1 cup fresh trout meat, fully cooked

1 egg yolk, fully cooked

1-2 tablespoons broccoli, steamed and finely chopped

2 tablespoons sunflower oil

Steps

1. In a food processor, add everything together. Puree until blended.

2. Serve immediately for best taste, but it can be stored in the fridge for 1-2 days with no ill effects.

Blended Mackerel

Like the trout smoothie above, this is more of a topper meal. My cats love mackerel, but it's not always great for them, so adding a bit to top their meals is the best way to make them extra happy without sacrificing their health.

Ingredients

1 cup canned mackerel in oil

1 tablespoon sunflower oil

1 tablespoon cooked brown rice

2 tablespoons no-salt chicken broth or plain filtered watered

Steps

1. Take your mackerel and carefully pat it with paper towels to remove the oils. You don't have to get all of it off, but the bulk should be removed.

2. Add all the ingredients into a food processor and blend until smooth, adding the broth a little at a time to get a nice consistency.

3. Serve immediately for best taste, or package and store for 1-2 days.

Kitty Pasta

I got the idea for this recipe when Babs stole a few noodles from my unobserved dish a few years ago. My cats really enjoy this pasta dish as a treat, and I probably make it once a month for dinner when salmon goes on sale.

Not every cat will love pasta, so know your cat's preferences before you try it!

Ingredients

1 pound salmon fillet, boneless

1 cup small pasta, whole grain

¼ cup frozen spinach, thawed and well-drained

2-3 tablespoons shredded cheddar cheese, optional

3 tablespoons kelp powder

¼ teaspoon lite salt

½ teaspoon bone meal

100 mg taurine

Steps

1. Preheat your oven to 400. Line a baking sheet with parchment paper.

2. Place your salmon skin side down and bake for 10-15 minutes, or until cooked through. You can also air fry at 400 for 7-10 minutes.

3. Meanwhile, bring a medium pot of water to boil. Add your pasta.

4. Cook, stirring occasionally until pasta is cooked according to directions, usually about 10 minutes. Drain.

5. In the bowl of a food processor, combine your pasta, spinach, cheese, bone meal, taurine, lite salt, and kelp powder. Pulse until it is mostly broken down.

6. Flake your salmon in the processor and pulse until thoroughly combined.

7. Cool to room temperature before serving.

Salmon Meals

This only has a bit of salmon, but the organ meat is wildly healthy, so it's a great recipe for those cats who just love seafood.

Ingredients

50 grams chicken liver, raw

50 grams beef kidney, raw

1.5-2 cups water, as needed

100 grams chicken heart, raw

700 grams chicken wings, raw, with bones and skin

100 grams salmon, raw, with bones

1 teaspoon taurine

Steps

1. Chop your organ meat into small to medium pieces. With a sharp cleaver, cut through the chicken wings into manageable pieces. Place everything in a bowl.

2. Toss with taurine powder and place in the freezer for 15-20 minutes to set up.

3. Grind your semi-frozen meat and organ mixture.

4. Add 1.5 cups of water and mix very well using your hands to work the liquid in. If it does not come together in a cohesive mixture, add more water a little at a time until it does.

5. Portion and store until ready to consume.

Chicken and Tuna Combo

This is another very easy meal to throw together, and my cats love it. Once again, it falls under special treat meal and is not something to feed them every single day due to the metals in tuna. This makes several small portions as well, so they're great for topping meals.

Ingredients

1 can of tuna packed in water, drained very well

½ cup brown rice, cooked

¼ cup chicken liver, cooked

Steps

1. Place your chicken liver in a food processor and blend until very smooth. You can add a small amount of water or no-sodium chicken broth if it struggles to come together.

2. Dump your blended livers in a medium bowl. Add your tuna and brown rice.

3. Mix well, and then form into several small 'nuggets' or balls for your cat. With this amount, I can usually make between 7-8 balls.

4. Serve immediately, or portion and store until ready to consume.

TREATS, AN OVERVIEW

Treats are not just something you give your cat when training or as a special moment. Treats can be something small and extra to their diet or just something of a bonus to their normal routine. Some of these treats are exactly what you think of when you think of treats, but others are simply 'bonus' snacks to keep them happy and healthy.

As always, keep in mind your cat's caloric daily intake before feeding treats, and never feed them excessively. Responsible feeding leads to healthy, happy cats.

Cat Omelet

This is actually a great way to start your cat's day! While it's true cats can't handle a lot of dairy, this recipe has a ton of good fat and protein. If your cat can handle small amounts of dairy (both of mine can!), this could be a recipe in regular rotation for you.

Ingredients

3 eggs

1 tablespoon shredded carrot

1 tablespoon shredded zucchini

1 tablespoon non-fat dried milk

2-3 tablespoons cottage cheese

Steps

1. In a medium bowl, add your non-fat milk powder and the appropriate amount of water to rehydrate. It's usually about a teaspoon or two, but every brand has different instructions, so be sure to follow your specific instructions. Mix well.

2. Crack 3 eggs in the bowl with the milk and mix well.

3. Heat a nonstick skillet over medium heat. If needed, you can add a small amount of oil, but if your skillet is really nonstick, you shouldn't need it.

4. Pour your entire egg mixture into the pan as if you were making an omelet or large pancake.

5. Let cook undisturbed for 4-5 minutes, or until the egg pancake is set well on the bottom and about 55% cooked.

6. Flip your egg pancake completely so the other side can cook. If you struggle with it, you can slide the egg onto a plate, hold your skillet upside down over the plate, and flip everything over.

7. On the mostly cooked side, place your shredded vegetables and then spread the cottage cheese across the top.

8. Let cook fully. Allow to cool some before cutting into bite-sized pieces and offering it warm to your cat. Portion and store any remaining portions.

Cat Salad

In the wild, cats actually eat greens. It makes sense, considering how plentiful that supply is. Would they prefer to eat meat? Sure, but they'll happily take what they can get. As you are probably aware, greens are also very healthy with a ton of nutrients. If your cat has an interest, this salad is packed with nutrients and absolutely delicious.

Ingredients

¼ cup zucchini, grated

½ cup alfalfa sprouts, chopped finely

1/8 cup no-salt chicken or fish stock*

Fresh catnip, for garnish

*My cats far prefer fish stock for this recipe, but finding any fish stock, let alone fish stock without salt, can be hard. If you can't find it, chicken or even turkey is a good substitute.

Steps

1. Set out your grated zucchini and alfalfa sprouts on a cutting board and chop finely. Add this to a small bowl.

2. Toss with your stock. Top with a small amount of minced catnip for added interest, and serve.

Salmon Crunchies

This is more in line of a traditional treat. I've not only made this recipe probably a hundred times, but I've also made this recipe for countless friends and family members who have cats. It always goes over well.

Ingredients

1 can of salmon packed in water, 10 ounces, undrained

1 whole egg

2 cups whole wheat flour

Steps

1. Preheat your oven to 350 degrees. Line a baking tray with parchment paper and set aside.

2. Dump your can of salmon into a food processor with all the liquid. Process until it is chopped very finely.

3. In a stand mixer or a large bowl, place your 1 egg, chopped salmon, and 1.5 cups of whole wheat flour. Mix well until everything comes together. You want a tacky dough, not a sticky dough. You can continue to add flour into the dough until you get that tacky texture if it is too wet.

4. Lightly flour your work surface and turn your dough out. Lightly flour your rolling pin and roll your dough out to about a quarter of an inch thickness.

5. Cut your treats out. I use a ¾ inch cookie cutter that looks like little fish, but you can use any small cutter you have or just cut squares out with a paring knife. Some people use a pizza cutter to

cut long, even lines and cuts easily. Transfer your treats onto your baking sheet lined with parchment paper.

6. Bake for 20 minutes, or until starting to brown and crispy.

7. Let cool before treating your cat or storing in an airtight container for up to 3 weeks.

Cranberry Oat Treats

Cranberries are very healthy, and some studies have suggested they can help prevent UTIs. However, cats generally aren't clamoring to eat cranberries plain. These treats use dried cranberries for all the benefits, plus some added catnip to get your cats really interested.

Ingredients

1 cup rolled oats

4 tablespoons dried cranberries*

½ cup cooked chicken

2 tablespoons coconut oil

1 generous tablespoon catnip

1 egg

*Be careful of the cranberries you buy! Most dried cranberries have a lot of extra sugar added, which you don't need. You want cranberries with just cranberries as the ingredients. If you can't find this, you can dehydrate your own.

Steps

1. Preheat your oven to 350 degrees. Line a baking sheet with parchment paper and set aside.

2. Chop your chicken into small, manageable pieces.

3. In a small bowl or on the stove, heat your coconut oil until it becomes liquid.

4. In a food processor, place your oats and blend until it becomes a flour consistency.

5. Add in your cranberries, and pulse again until they are finely ground. They may clump a little more than the oats, but that is fine.

6. Add everything else, including the egg and catnip, to the processor and pulse again until it has all come together. If it's a little too dry and crumbly, your egg may be a bit small – add water, a teaspoon at a time, until it forms into a dough.

7. Using a ¼ teaspoon, scoop out treat-sized dollops and roll into balls. Press each ball flat on your parchment paper.

8. Bake for 15-20 minutes, or until golden brown. Let cool completely before offering it to your cat or storing it in an airtight container in the fridge for up to a week.

Tuna Catnip Delight

Who doesn't love tuna? This recipe is similar to our previous one but uses regular all-purpose flour and tuna instead of salmon. Many of you may already have all these ingredients in the pantry anyway!

Ingredients

1 can, 4 ounces, of tuna packed in water, undrained

1 cup all-purpose flour

1 egg

2 tablespoons dried catnip

Steps

1. Preheat your oven to 350 degrees. Line a baking sheet with parchment paper and set aside.

2. Place your tuna in a food processor with all the water it was packed with. Process until the tuna has broken down.

3. Add your flour, egg, and catnip. Pulse until it comes together in a dough.

4. Using a ¼ teaspoon measuring spoon, form your dough into small balls and set them on your parchment-lined baking sheet. Slightly flatten each ball into a round treat shape.

5. Bake for 15-18 minutes, or until golden brown and crispy. Let cool before offering it to your cat or storing it in an airtight container for a week.

Carrot Treats

If your kitty struggles with its veggie intake, this recipe is a good option. It uses carrot as the main ingredient and has lots of good fats, along with some protein, to round out any kitty's diet.

Ingredients

2 tablespoons coconut oil

1.5 cups whole wheat flour

1 tablespoon dried catnip

¾ cup carrot, finely shredded (use the small holes on a box grater!)

1 egg

Steps

1. Preheat your oven to 375 degrees. Line a baking tray with parchment paper and set aside.

2. In a small bowl in the microwave or over low heat, melt your coconut oil until it becomes liquid.

3. In a stand mixer or a medium bowl, add 1 cup of your flour and the melted coconut oil. Mix until it appears sandy and no large chunks of oil remain.

4. Add your catnip and finely shredded carrots, and mix well.

5. Finally, add your egg. Mix again. You should have a smooth, tacky dough. If it is too dry and crumbly, add a little bit of water or no-sodium vegetable broth a tablespoon at a time. If it's too wet and loose, add a bit more of your flour to thicken it up.

6. Once you get a smooth dough mixture, flour your workspace and turn your dough out.

7. Flour your rolling pin and roll the dough out to about a quarter of an inch, using flour as needed, so nothing sticks.

8. From here, you can use a small ¾ inch cookie cutter to cut your treats or simply a paring knife. I have seen folks use a pizza cutter for ease of cutting, which also works well.

9. Lay out your treats on your baking sheet.

10. Bake for 12-15 minutes, or until they are golden brown and starting to crisp.

11. Cool completely before offering to your cat or storing in an airtight container for up to two weeks.

Hairball Prevention Treats

In a perfect world, your cats wouldn't struggle at all with hairballs. However, most of us don't live in a perfect world. If your cat has long, luxurious fur and struggles with its hairballs, these treats are for you. The oil and pumpkin both help keep things moving and will allow your cat to process and pass their hair faster instead of upchucking it onto your just-cleaned rug or bedspread.

Ingredients

1.5 cups whole wheat flour

1/3 cup canned pumpkin puree*

1 egg

2 tablespoons ground flax seed

3 tablespoons coconut oil

1-2 tablespoons no sodium vegetable broth or water, as needed

1 tablespoon catnip

*Make sure you purchase and use just pumpkin puree, not the pie filling. They are often in the same section of the store and look

similar, so read the ingredients. You want only pumpkin as the ingredient, with no spices, sugars, or additives.

Steps

1. Preheat your oven to 350 degrees.

2. In a small bowl or on the stovetop, heat your coconut oil until liquid.

3. Place all ingredients in the bowl of a stand mixer or a large bowl, including your liquid oil. Mix well until everything comes together in a dough.

4. Cover and let rest for 5-10 minutes. This will hydrate the flour.

5. Lay out a piece of parchment paper. Turn your dough onto the parchment paper and knead a few times to loosen up.

6. Lightly flour a rolling pin and roll your dough to about a quarter of an inch thickness.

7. Using a paring knife or a pizza cutter, cut your dough into a grid pattern.

8. Transfer the whole piece of parchment paper to a baking tray. Bake for about 10 minutes.

9. Remove the tray from the oven. With heatproof gloves or pot holders, break up your grid of semi-cooked treats into individual ones. Spread them evenly onto the tray and put them back into the oven for 10-15 minutes.

10. Remove from oven when brown and fully firm. Let cool completely before offering to your cat or storing in an airtight container for up to three weeks.

DEHYDRATED MEAT TREATS 101

The purest and whole food source you can offer your cats for a treat is just meat, nothing extra or fancy. There are a few ways you can do this, but by far, the easiest is to use a dehydrator.

There are several types of dehydrators on the market and hundreds of brands to choose from. It can be overwhelming, but if you have interested in doing this or using your dehydrator for other things (like making homemade jerky for yourself, dehydrating fruits or vegetables, etc.), picking up one could be well worth the money and research. I have personally had great luck getting second-hand dehydrators on resale marketplaces online or even at estate sales or thrift stores.

If you don't have a dehydrator, you may be able to use your oven at the lowest setting or an air fryer!

This is a blank, easy recipe to help you understand the basics. Use whatever meat you like in portions that make sense for your cats!

Ingredients

1-2 pounds of raw meat of your choice

Steps

1. Slice your meat against the grain (for maximum tenderness) in thin slices, between 1 and 2 inches long. They will shrink while they cook and dehydrate, so make them slightly larger than you think they should be.

2. Place your meat slices on your dehydrator trays. You don't want anything touching; make sure there is space for air circulation. If you're doing this in your oven, use a baking tray with a rack to raise the meats to allow for circulation.

3. Place in your dehydrator at a temperature of 155-165 degrees. Let dehydrate for several hours.

4. After about 5 hours, start checking your meat. You want it to be dry all the way through and bend but not snap when you go to bend it with your hands. Depending on your dehydrator and how thick you cut the meat, it may be done in 5 hours. For others, it could take up to 7.

5. Let cool completely before storing in an airtight container in a cool, dark place for a week, in the fridge for 2-3 weeks, or in the freezer for several months.

Health Note:

This should go without saying, but I am going to reiterate that these are treats, not meal replacements. Something to remember with these treats specifically is that dried meats will rehydrate when exposed to liquid… like the liquid in a cat's stomach. Only give a small amount at a time, especially for smaller cats.

Suggested Alternative Meats

My cats will never turn down a piece of dried beef from a roast or a chunk of chicken. However, don't limit yourself this way! The liver, heart, and even lungs of animals can be dehydrated in this same way for healthy, tasty treats that provide a ton of nutrients. Small shrimp or chunks of larger shrimp, slices of salmon or trout… the potential is endless here.

THE QUESTIONS YOU MAY NEED TO HAVE ANSWERED

If you have come this far and still have questions, or concerns, never fear! Many people do. These are some of the common questions I run into after working with people to create a meal plan for their cats.

"Do I need to feed exclusively raw or exclusively commercial?"

Great question! Some people think that doing a half and half diet is something that may be right for them, as in, a single meal of raw or homemade food and then another meal with commercial foods. Technically, you absolutely could do this. I don't necessarily recommend it, however.

The problem is that the recipes in this book, and the recipes you're going to find online, generally provide all the nutrients your cat needs with the assumption that this is what they are eating. The nutrition values in commercial foods could be different, so your cat may accidentally be missing something if you are mixed feeding.

The only way in my mind this could work is if you stick with pure grinding instead of a frankenprey method. That way, each portion has exactly the nutrients and vitamins for that meal specifically. However, there are still risks with not getting everything in a single meal.

If you really want to do mixed feedings, it can be done, but it isn't as foolproof as doing just one or just the other. If you're already prepping meals, it's not that much more work to prep all the meals for the week or even the month.

"How can we travel with this meal schedule?!"

This is the biggest long-term concern a see with a lot of cat owners, and I get it! It's not like you can schedule an auto-feeder to dispense ground beef or chunks of chicken.

Traveling takes more prep work and planning, but it absolutely can be done. My husband and I hire a pet sitter we found recommended in a local community group. She comes twice a day while we are gone and feeds Babs and DD, plus gives them some love, makes sure they have water, and waters my plants.

Everything is labeled in the kitchen, and I usually print out a chart I stick to the fridge that says who gets what meals and when. Before her first weekend away with us, I walked her through a typical feeding, showed her where they eat, and it wasn't ever a problem. If needed for longer trips, I have extra meals frozen that she can (with instruction!) pull out the night before, so there are no worries about longer trips.

If you don't have someone in your community group to trust, apps like Rover and Wag exist that you can work through. Thoroughly vet whoever you have looking after your pet, though, look through their reviews, and find someone you are comfortable with. I know many vet techs and other professionals use these sites for extra cash, and that would be the ideal 'stranger' to bring into your home – someone that knows animals.

You don't necessarily need to pay a stranger, though. If you have family members who can cat sit, or even a niece or nephew looking to make extra money that you trust, they may be a good option for you. Some folks have also had great luck with boarding facilities and cats, which is certainly an option if you feel more comfortable.

With a boarding facility, just be sure to ask the right questions and let them know you do feed raw. Some facilities may not be able to store the food for you properly, and others may not be comfortable with raw food due to their lack of knowledge or experience handling it. It's a great learning opportunity for them, but only if they are willing and receptive.

Ultimately, it's just important to find someone you trust.

"Where do I buy the meats?"

I've touched on this previously in the book, but it's still such a common question I see. Most people think that if they aren't buying Whole Foods 1000% Organic, Naturally Raised meats, there is no point in doing it. That's not at all true!

You can buy your meat anywhere you would be comfortable buying it for yourself. That could include your corner grocery store, your local grocery chain, or an actual butcher shop. You can buy your meat on sale or from the cheapest seller. As long as it's still good quality meat and you follow all best buy dates and safety guidelines, this is fine.

In short: buy where you want, and don't stress too much about it!

"I'm so confused: aren't bones bad?!"

I'm sure you have heard about bones splintering and breaking in an animal's mouth, causing damage to their teeth, gums, or internal organs. It's scary to think about, and what's worse is that many bones that can do this are on the market right now.

The fact, though, is that this really only applies to cooked bones. Bones that have been cooked are much more brittle, as the cooking process sucks a lot of the moisture and nutrients from the bone. Dry, brittle, cooked bones can splinter and cause harm.

Raw bones, though, provide no risk. Raw chicken bones, for example, are so soft that your cat can and often will eat through them. It provides incredible nutrients and is a building block for a good cat diet.

In short: cooked bones = bad.

Raw bones = good!

"This doesn't seem like enough food!"

I see many new food makers overfeeding their cats because the portions are, admittedly, smaller than commercial food. While your cat may only get a quarter cup to half cup of food a meal, depending on the recipe, they are used to getting a cup or two of dry food.

Raw food is significantly more efficient. There are no fillers, nothing 'excessive' in the food, and there's no reason for them to eat more! Their caloric and nutritional needs are met in a much smaller portion overall. Don't stress if it doesn't look like enough food. As long as they are full and meeting their caloric goals (while not losing or gaining weight!), you are perfectly fine.

"Should my cat's food be grain-free?"

There are a ton of buzzwords about grain-free diets floating around the internet right now. I believe I have done an excellent job explaining why your cat needs some grains in their diet and providing some recipes that utilize that.

The truth is that there are not a ton of scientific studies at the moment that go into the advantages, or disadvantages, of a grain-free diet for a cat. There are, however, several emerging studies that show grain-free diets are not healthy for dogs and can lead to heart problems and early death.

Scary? It is!

Similar studies are yet to be performed on cats, but it's important to provide a balanced diet, which can include some grains. They should never be the main ingredient, but in my opinion, and many vet's opinions, it is a 'better safe than sorry' situation.

"My cat has allergies; what do I do?!"

It's rare, but some cats have allergies that might make these recipes seem useless to you. The most common and frustrating allergy I've run into is an allergy to chicken in cats.

In this situation, simply substitute with another type of poultry. Turkey is a great swap and is very healthy for your cat. If they also react to them, beef or pork are also both great options.

Even if your cat has allergies, they can absolutely still enjoy a homemade diet. Just be careful when feeding them new foods, and never intentionally feed them anything they are allergic to!

"But I'm worried I won't be perfect."

That's a real concern, and I have spent thousands of words within this book instilling how important vitamins and balance are for you and your cat's life. Many owners don't take the leap because they're worried about not being 100% perfect.

Here's a hot take, though: neither are the commercial foods you buy. Dry food doesn't have nearly enough moisture for a cat's diet to keep them healthy. More housecats are overweight than ever before, and there seems to be a growing diabetes issue with cats that may be directly linked to commercial foods.

Labeling regulations are questionable as well. In order for cat food to be labeled as "complete and balanced," it has to follow certain testing guidelines, which include studying a cat over the course of six months that is exclusively fed this diet. The study follows 8 cats, but 2 are allowed to drop out, so really, 6 cats. At the end of the 6 months, if they haven't lost 15% of their body weight and their bloodwork comes back fine, the label stays.

This is crazy! You're not only feeding your cat for six months, but for their life! Many issues with a cat's diet may not show up in bloodwork until it has reached a critical point.

Your homemade diet may not be perfect, but as long as you focus on the nutrients and try, you won't be doing worse than what you could buy in the store.

There are also some questions that come after folks start and get the hang of this.

"My cat's bowel movements are different!"

Well, of course, they are. You just changed their diet!

If your cat is experiencing stomach discomfort or issues during the transition process, you may be transitioning too quickly. Slow down some, and go with a slower and easier introduction to homemade food.

If your cat is fully on this diet and you're concerned they're constipated… are you sure? Homemade diets like this are amazing because your cat utilizes nearly every part. That means it can be completely normal, depending on the caloric intake and the cat, for them to not have a bowel movement every single day.

Signs of constipation include straining without anything happening, diarrhea, excessive grooming of the behind, and potentially going to the bathroom outside of the litter box. If your cat is experiencing these symptoms, consider adding more water to their meals and reducing the bone content, which could be causing constipation. If it persists, talk to your vet, as it could be an indication of an underlying condition.

However, if your cat has normal, mostly dry bowel movements with little odor, you're doing something right.

"How often should I be feeding my cat?"

Generally, I recommend those who feed their cats homemade food a feeding schedule of twice a day, once in the morning and once at night. This gives your cat plenty of time to digest between meals and offers a good balance. Divide their caloric intake into two, and each meal should have that.

If your cat is very large, you can break it up into three meals a day if you prefer, but I find getting home during the workweek for the lunch feeding can be a struggle.

It may be an adjustment if your cat is used to 'free feeding' dry food, but don't let those dramatic meows fool you. They aren't starving, just upset their routine has changed!

"My cat won't eat it all at once!"

This is fairly common. A lot of cats prefer to graze throughout the day instead of eating a full meal in a sitting. As long as they aren't letting their raw food sit out for hours and hours at a time, potentially growing bacteria, it is completely safe.

Be sure, though, that this isn't because you're overfeeding your cat! If they often go until their next mealtime with food left, you may want to recalculate their calories.

LAST WORDS

If you have made it this far, it seems that you are really dedicated to making your own cat food, and I applaud you! As you probably realize by now, it's not an easy or simple process. It takes time, dedication, and focus, especially at first.

It also takes a good relationship with your cat. They need to trust you, and you need to be paying attention to them and their habits so you know for sure how they are handling the dietary changes.

It's totally okay if this journey isn't for you; there is no shame. But I do believe with proper research and knowledge, like what you have gained through these pages, it can be for many people. It doesn't have to be complicated, overwhelming, or hard. A little trial and error and some recipes under your belt, and there is a good chance you will agree with me, too.

Printed in Dunstable, United Kingdom